Harry Anderson

Harry Anderson

PHOTO BY JOHN MC CARTHY

Harry Anderson

The Man Behind the Paintings
Raymond H. Woolsey and Ruth Anderson

Review and Herald Publishing Association
Washington, D.C. 20012

Copyright © 1976 by
Review and Herald Publishing Association

Library of Congress Catalog Card No. 76-15700

Editor: Thomas A. Davis
Design, cover, and line drawings: Elfred Lee

Printed in U.S.A.

CONTENTS

ILLUSTRATIONS

Harry Anderson Paintings That Appear in This Book

*Reproduced in Color

ACKNOWLEDGMENTS

Appreciation is expressed to the following, who own copyrights to respective illustrations in this book:

Collier's Magazine, pp. 23, 28, 60.

Nabisco, Inc., p. 27.

Tim Anderson, pp. 40, 41.

Woman's Home Companion Magazine, p. 80.

John Hancock Mutual Life Insurance Company, p. 88.

American Artist Magazine, p. 89.

New York Center, p. 62.

Corporation of the President of The Church of Jesus Christ of Latter-day Saints, pp. 101, 106, 120, 122, 123.

Harry Anderson and Samuel L. Feldman, p. 110.

Exxon Corporation, pp. 114, 115.

(All other paintings and illustrations are copyrighted by Review and Herald Publishing Association.)

FOREWORD

Not all heroes are those who sacrifice their lives in some daring feat. There are innumerable heroes who live quiet, everyday lives. To me, my husband is such a person.

The test of one's courage often may be the way he faces the grind of daily routine. I have seen Harry endure a sometimes brutally monotonous existence. I have marveled at his dedication and faithfulness to his work in a lonely studio, year after year.

He is concerned only with true values. Neither social position nor material possessions hold his interest. In him I find strength, security, and a sense of permanence. What more can one expect of a hero?

—Ruth Anderson

A MAN
CALLED HARRY

Two automobiles turned off a back-country road in southern New England on a recent summer evening and followed a curving driveway up to the kitchen door of a two-story frame house. The lead car was a sleek and shiny limousine, complete with liveried chauffeur. The other car was a Rolls Royce, driven by its owner. In the house Harry and Ruth Anderson had just finished supper. They were not expecting visitors.

In answer to the knock, Harry opened the door to find a friend, Wendell Ashton, who introduced his companions, J. Willard Marriott, whom Harry knew to be the head of a multimillion-dollar business complex, including motels and food services, and Hobart Lewis, editor in chief of *Reader's Digest.* Ashton is worldwide director of public communications for the Church of Jesus Christ of Latter-day Saints.

Ruth was dismayed. She hurried into the living room ahead of the guests to tidy up a bit, stuff magazines away and straighten pillows on the couch. But it was precisely the homey atmosphere of the Anderson house that Ashton wanted his companions to see—that and to meet Harry himself.

Marriott was gracious, and Lewis was entranced by Harry's three-foot wooden model of a sailing vessel. But the visitors didn't stay in the house long. "Show us your studio, Harry," Marriott urged. Harry Anderson is always quietly amused when anyone asks to see his studio. It's a workshop, really, and not just where he produces his paintings. It is also where he sews, carves, creates models, makes picture frames, and builds furniture. It is not a showcase and is usually untidy.

The three men admired the half-finished picture on Harry's easel—a scene from the life of Christ—and were gone.

The postman brought a letter bearing a stamp from the Island of Papua in the South Pacific. It was from a Seventh-day Adventist mission there. "Your pictures have proved so great an inspiration to all of us—Europeans and nationals alike. . . . Your pictures are doing our souls good, and we greatly desire that the Lord will continue to use you as a preacher of righteousness to so many."

The book editor of a large religious publishing house declared unequivocally, "I can identify with Christ better in Harry Anderson's pictures than through those of any other artist. When I see an Anderson rendition of Jesus it says to me, This truly was the Son of God. He loves me and I love Him.

"There's an old story that a portrait of the crucified Christ was being exhibited in a small country town. Unlike many such portraits, His eyes were open, full of infinite pity, and looking straight at the beholder. Many people were looking at the picture, silently, intensely. A man in the front row, forgetting his surroundings, absorbed in the painting, whispered, 'I love Him.' Another, standing nearby, heard him and whispered also, 'Yes, I love Him too!' The words were repeated from person to person; every heart was stirred.

"I don't know which picture that was, or who the artist was, but I feel that Harry Anderson's paintings of Christ stir the same emotions—I know they do in my heart."

On the embossed stationery of the Royal Palace, Hashemite Kingdom of Jordan, the king's secretary inquires about the price if Harry Anderson were to do a painting of the king. The Jordanians had seen his work in the *Ladies' Home Journal* and admired his style.

From the wife of an art director:
"Dear Mr. Anderson: This is a letter of both praise and thanks. I recently purchased for my two small children a reproduction of your picture *What Happened to*

Your Hand? and it means more than I can tell you to our entire family—one of the first things my 5-year-old son shows off to his 'buddies,' when they come in, is the picture of his 'Jesus.'

"I spent several months looking in art dealers' shops for a picture that would express just what I wanted my children to feel about the living Christ. I looked at dozens of sepias and very fine reproductions of old masters— *Madonna and Child,* et cetera, which, though lovely, were not real and personal to small children. When I saw yours, I knew it was just what I wanted. The color, the reverence, the composition, and the feeling of Jesus as being alive to children of today—is perfectly done. It portrays to us Jesus as not reserved for small children of Biblical times in foreign surroundings, but for my children here and now.

"I am a graduate in fine arts. I painted portraits before my marriage, and my husband is a practicing artist, both easel and commercial; he is an art director. So your work has been well known to us for many years and has always had our joint respect and admiration.

"Many thanks for conceiving a picture that my children can love and grow up with."

For most of his forty-five years of illustrating and gallery painting Harry has been recognized as one of the nation's topmost artists. When national magazines such as *Collier's, Saturday Evening Post, Woman's Home Companion,* and the current *Ladies' Home Journal* and *Good Housekeeping,* were in their heyday, Harry Anderson illustrations and covers were among their regular features. But about 50 per cent of his work has been in the field of religious illustrating, and these pictures have been reproduced by the millions around the globe.

It was here also that he made what was perhaps his most unique contribution—he and his art director pioneered the idea of portraying Jesus Christ in traditional flowing white robes but in modern settings, with modern-day children at play, with modern grownups at work or in their homes or gardens. The impact of such pictures is that Jesus is indeed in "the here and now."

Probably most admirers of Harry Anderson's work would agree with the religious-book editor, that their chief point of identification is in the personality that comes across in the figure of Christ. Here is depicted poise with a total lack of self-consciousness; tenderness, love, and pity, without a trace of weakness. Appeal seems to almost pour out of His eyes, yet it is obviously based on a position of strength, both physical and moral. This is written in His stance, in His bearing, in His gestures. Strength and love, power and pity, justice and mercy—these attributes in combination practically define deity. Theologians consume volumes trying to spell it out in words—to portray it in a painting indeed requires the hand of a master.

Superb skill as a craftsman and a deeply intimate relationship with his Subject—that is what one would expect of the artist upon seeing a Harry Anderson painting. So meeting the man in person may be a rather disconcerting experience, for he might not fit most people's idea of an artist—and may even intimidate some people. His six-

An idea
is born.

foot frame is made to seem even larger by broad shoulders, barrel chest, and slim hips, suggestive of an ex-football player who has taken care of his body.

What do an artist's hands look like? Harry's can be described only as heavy, with thick fingers. They look like those of a farmer or a bricklayer. It is almost inconceivable that those rough hands can evoke all shades of human emotions with the deft stroke of a brush.

A jutting chin and strong nose accentuate the craggy features of his face. A high forehead ends in a bit of wispy hair on the top of his head. There is more hair on the sides of his head, but it has turned gray, for he is entering his seventh decade. Harry has a tendency to lower his face and pin his subject with deeply set eyes—one blue and one green—staring from beneath beetling, bushy brows. This look seems almost belligerent until his face breaks into a lopsided grin. The lines in his face his wife calls "character marks," and his indisposing mien doubtless comes from a lifelong habit of studying carefully whatever he sees.

A second look at Harry Anderson, in an attempt to judge his personality, is likely to center on an entirely different aspect and is likely to be as incorrect as the first one. He doesn't say much, and only by careful questioning can he be drawn into talking about himself or his work. This might be interpreted as introversion, aloofness, or even as arrogance, depending on the observer. Both of Harry's parents were Swedish, so some of his reticence can be accounted for simply as his cultural heritage. His feelings are deep, and while there may be some shyness there, again he may be occupied with things different from most people. He is constantly observing and photographing in his mind such phenomena as the play of light across a face. Further, as a lifelong student of human emotions he can quickly take the measure of a person's character. He may be studying his interviewer more accurately than his interviewer is studying him.

What does it take to make a top-flight artist of the son of an immigrant metalworker? What sort of experience would alter the career of a national illustrator to devote so much of his life to religious painting? What strange alchemy of spirit moves on a man's soul that from the

15

depths of a cluttered studio he can send forth a painting that will preach thousands of silent sermons every day?

Skill comes from practice; practice comes from determination; and in the final analysis, determination comes from the inner wellsprings of a person's individuality where he looks at himself and says, You are you; God has made only one of you. Let us see what you can do.

In the beginning, as the high-water mark of His creation, God made man, saying, "Let us make man in our image." Many people feel that man comes closest to being like his Creator when he is creative, when he gives vent to the powers that surge up within him, producing ideas, objects, relationships, that had never existed before. And this creation, in turn, enriches all humanity, to the glory of the original Creator.

16

THE MAKING
OF AN ARTIST

Harry Anderson's father, Joseph, immigrated to the
United States from Sweden, alone, at the age of 12. (That
would make an interesting book, in itself.) He found a
job and, upon growing to manhood, married Clara Stahl,
a Swedish girl, and settled in a small frame house in Chicago's Westside. To them were born one daughter and
three sons. The three boys very closely resembled one
another, bearing their father's strong lips, nose, chin, and
dark-set eyes.

The children were named largely after their parents,
and so they used their middle names—Clara Josephine,
John Clarence, Joseph Harry, and Carl William. Harry,
born August 11, 1906, was the next to the youngest, yet
grew to be the tallest. Like good little Swedes, they were
all tow-headed until they reached maturity, when their
hair darkened. An early picture of Harry shows him lined
up with his cousins, his cap turned sidewise and one foot
turned askew. This latter proved to be a lifelong trait—
he works standing at his easel, often with one foot turned
or resting on the other.

Mr. Anderson was a sheet-metal worker; for forty
years he was connected with a firm that manufactured
coal-burning furnaces. Mrs. Anderson surrounded her
children with love and consistent firmness. She was both
thrifty and a wonderful cook. Although they grew up under modest circumstances, her children were never aware
of the lack of money. Theirs was a strong and secure family, happy with what they had. Mrs. Anderson was a
staunch Lutheran and a strong disciplinarian. She in-
stilled in her children high ideals and inspired them al-

Harry as a small boy.

ways to do their best at whatever they undertook.

All of the children made good grades, especially in mathematics. Josephine became a treasurer in the Denver school system; Clarence, after studying engineering, designed hydroturbines and other facilities for the Federal Government. William was an officer in the Internal Revenue Service. The government sent him on overseas assignments to help foreign governments set up computer systems to handle their tax-collecting programs.

So when Harry enrolled at the University of Illinois, in 1925, he chose to study math also. He didn't have much money for a college career, but in those days it didn't take much—seventy-seven dollars would pay for a semester's tuition. He took his meals in a private home that catered to students, and he earned his keep by washing dishes and waiting on tables. During the summer, to earn a bit of cash toward his tuition, Harry tried his hand at selling hosiery. That job was a failure, and he pieced out the summer at odd jobs—cutting lawns, landscaping, whatever he could find.

In registering for his sophomore year, Harry had to choose an elective to complete his curriculum. He

18

wanted a "pipe" course to balance the tough math courses required, so he chose a class in still-life painting. (So simply is a person's destiny altered.) As he plodded through the fall term and into the spring, he began to wonder just what future a mathematics major held for him. The prospects looked pretty poor. Just about then his art professor told Harry his work showed considerably more talent than the usual art student.

"Have you ever given serious consideration to art as a profession?" he asked. Young Anderson enjoyed his art class—it certainly was a diversion from the other courses —but he hadn't realized his work showed that much potential. No one in his family, as far back as he knew, had shown talent along that line.

The only previous experience young Anderson had had in painting—if such it could be called—was during a couple of years after high school that he had spent working in a large stationery store on Chicago's Loop. He had begun the job as a stock boy. The store had a contract with a man who painted the signs and markers and display notices used throughout the store—"Special Discount," "50 Per Cent Off Today Only," et cetera. One day this

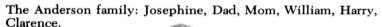

The Anderson family: Josephine, Dad, Mom, William, Harry, Clarence.

19

man could not meet an order deadline and Harry suggested to the store management that he could do it. His work was satisfactory, so he was given the job permanently. He set up a shop on the store's fourth floor and did all the signs for the entire store.

The art instructor at the University of Illinois was a graduate of Syracuse School of Art, and recommended that school to Harry. He enrolled in the freshman class in 1927. Here again he made expenses by waiting on tables, along with odd jobs of lettering and sign painting.

At Syracuse the emphasis of instruction was on basic drawing. As a freshman, Harry did nothing but practice and practice some more, drawing from plaster casts of famous statues: works by Michelangelo, Rodin, and others. He became almost sick of plaster casts, but this elementary instruction drilled into him lessons of proportion and perspective.

In his second year, classes on human anatomy were added to his curriculum—he had to learn every bone and muscle as well as a medical student did. Now Harry feels sorry for anyone attempting human figure drawing who has not had these basics. "It is really impossible," he says, "to make a clothed figure look realistic without a knowledge of what the body is doing underneath the clothes. Not only will the clothes not 'hang' right but the gestures and posture are likely to be stiff and off balance." Anderson didn't get into color theory and painting until his third and fourth years of school.

The quiet Swede was recognized as a leader among the thirty or so students in his class. In his lettering experience with opaque water colors he had a string to his bow the others lacked. (These paints look slightly different dry than wet, and so are harder to use.) Also, he'd taken that art course at Illinois. His friend Tom Lovell claimed he learned more from Anderson than from his teachers.

Harry's room was in the attic of his dormitory, but he and Lovell used a spare room on the second deck as their private studio. Besides doing their homework here, Harry earned pocket money at lettering jobs, and Tom received occasional assignments illustrating pulp magazines. In their senior year the two shared the post of art director of the yearbook for the entire university. Prestige was their only pay for a lot of hard work.

20

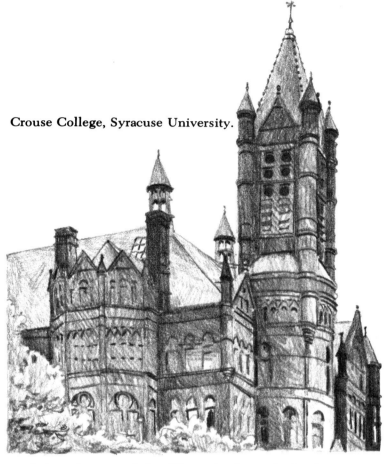

Crouse College, Syracuse University.

It is only natural that Harry Anderson's fondest memories of his years at Syracuse are in terms of the friendships he made there, rather than of the education itself. His classwork consisted largely of drill and drudgery, with little inspiration as far as the aesthetics of art were concerned. The school did not invite working illustrators in to lecture or demonstrate, although New York City was only two hundred miles away. Nor did the students make any field trips. The only contacts they had with the real world of art, as contrasted with the academic, were in periodic art shows held at the city library. These were conducted with no relationship to the university, but the art students sought them out—high spots in their learning experience. Harry and Tom learned to admire the way a picture was executed, not just the finished product alone.

The economic squeeze of the Depression was reflected in the resources available to the art students. A man hired as a model, for instance, had had no experience as such, but was a delivery man brought in off the street. He often went to sleep in the chair while posing for the class, not exactly inspiring as models go. Some of the

21

teachers themselves had had little experience out where art is bought and sold. Many of them had lived sheltered lives in the world of academe. Hibbard Kline, an instructor in illustration, stood out above the others. He had worked as an illustrator until a health problem developed and he came to Syracuse to teach. He was not a big talker like some of the other teachers, but he impressed his students with his warmth and sincerity.

As honor students, Harry and Tom could cut an unlimited number of classes, although they rarely took advantage of the privilege. But some of the classes really bothered Harry. One instructor insisted that he make a lot of little shapes on his canvas and color them in—with never a reason given for the exercise. The two friends decided to skip classes one day to play golf. But as they started across the campus they ran into Kline. They turned around and went back, not out of fear of reprisal but out of respect for this one teacher.

"Harry," Tom approached his friend one day, "what do you say we ditch this school business, go on down to New York, and get us a job."

Harry had to admit the idea had occurred to him. It didn't seem they were making any forward movement in their training—they had been doing plaster casts for years. But his own native doggedness, plus the fact his parents were eager for him to receive his degree, held him to the grind. Both men stuck it out and graduated with honors.

The pair wasted no time in getting to New York; they set up a studio in McDougall's Alley, just off Washington Square, along with other artist hopefuls. This alley paralleled fashionable Eighth Avenue. The carriage houses and stables on the alley had been turned into studios. Tom and Harry had one on a second floor. It was only eight feet wide and ran the length of the building, but it had a window facing north. Artists cherish a north light because it is the most constant natural light; windows facing other directions may let in direct sunlight or the light may change in color value as the sun moves from east to west across the sky.

This was the first illustration Harry Anderson did for a national magazine. It accompanied a "short-short, all-on-this-page" story in a 1932 issue of Collier's.

22

HARRY ANDERSON

It was just as well the men had not come to New York sooner, for in 1931 the economic depression lay heavily on the land, and the way of young artists was hard. They had been sheltered at Syracuse; they had known times were difficult, but they didn't realize just how hard until they had to try to make a living at their new profession. Harry found a job selling candy across the counter for the Mirror Candy Company. His post was at a branch store on Times Square, across the street from the Paramount Theater. His hours were from seven in the evening until two in the morning; patrons would stop by on their way to or from a show. Sometimes Anderson would help out at the soda fountain during the after-hour rush.

At ten dollars a week even this job didn't meet expenses. His food, eaten in restaurants, cost a dollar a day and his rent was twenty-five dollars a month. When he was promoted to night manager his salary was increased to twelve dollars, but that still didn't make ends meet— he even scrounged empty pop bottles for the pennies they would bring. He calls this his "starvation period." Fortunately, he had a considerate landlord who didn't dun him for his rent bill.

There was one compensation to the night job—it left his days free to paint and carry samples of his work around to the various art agencies, looking for a break into the field of his choice. He got several odd jobs, doing book jackets, which required a lot of lettering, something he had considerable experience in. Finally, April, 1932, Harry Anderson's big break came—*Collier's* magazine gave him a "short-short" story to illustrate and bought his picture of a French soldier coming home to his dog and his girl. It was in two-tone only—four-color work was too expensive in those depression years—and filled two columns.

Now the ice was broken. With that sale in his portfolio Anderson could approach other agencies with more confidence. "Nothing succeeds like success."

Harry gives credit to men like William Chessman, art director at *Collier's,* and Frank Eltonhead, who was at *Ladies' Home Journal* at the time, for helping him get his start. These men were willing to take hours from their busy schedule to help a struggling artist, to show him how to match a story with a picture, how a turn of a head or a tilt of a chin can intrigue a reader. "No man can

24

make his way in art alone," says Harry. "He must have help on the way. Many people do not realize that; from ignorance or pride they try to push ahead on their own and never really succeed at anything."

Harry was selling candy one night at the Times Square shop when a "spotter" came around, sent by the chain's main office to check up on personnel, sales conditions, and merchandise.

"The soda fountain is getting busy, Anderson. Move over there and help out," the spotter ordered.

"But sir, I have only this one pair of pants. That fountain work will ruin them."

"That's nothing to me. Get over there."

"In that case, you can have my job. I'm quitting." The spotter asked him to reconsider, but by putting in full time at his painting, Harry could now make more than the job's twelve dollars a week.

In two more years he had his backlog of debts paid off —his rent bill alone had climbed to five hundred dollars. Then he cleared out of New York and moved to Chicago. As he told Tom Lovell in farewell, he had had it, not just up to his neck but up to his eyebrows, with New York City.

A NEW FAMILY,
A NEW FAITH

In Chicago, Harry Anderson found a billet with Stevens-Gross, an art service agency that occupied the entire twenty-first floor of the Palmolive Building on Michigan Avenue. This agency had a stable of fourteen or fifteen artists, each supplied with a work area, materials, and any photos necessary from which to make his drawings. Two or three contact men made the rounds of advertising agencies and other art buyers. They would show samples of the artists' work, and the buyer would choose the type of work he wanted for his particular job. The average job, at the time Anderson joined Stevens-Gross, would pay around five hundred dollars. The artist would get half of this; the rest was shared by the studio and the contact man.

One of Anderson's first jobs in Chicago was the back cover, in color, for Montgomery Ward's big spring and summer catalog. If you've ever wondered how a seed catalog can show such perfect fruits and flowers, they are painted that way by an artist—or at least, that is what Harry did for Ward's.

Other big jobs followed in quick succession. A series of full-page ads for Cream of Wheat featured young boys full of pep and energy—with a dog and sled, fishing, prospecting. More ads included General Electric re-

A full-page advertisement for Cream of Wheat, one of a 1937 series. Other advertisement series by Anderson were for Wyeth Laboratories, Velveeta cheese, Coca-Cola, and Sealed Power piston rings.

26

Goin' Prospectin'

Dear Mom—
I've gone prospectin' for gold
to make us rich. I ate 2 bowls
of swell Cream of Wheat for breakfast
and I'm full up with food energy
Goodbye I may be gone a long time
Jimmy

P. S. Fix me another bowl of Cream of Wheat
for dinner tonight. Rover says goodbye too
I don't think he likes prospectin' like I do.

Make-believe adventure! There's one reason your youngster burns up terrific bodily energy each day. More than an adult in proportion to his size! Fortify him with hot Cream of Wheat for breakfast regularly. It's jam-packed with food energy that acts fast. Gets him off to a real start. Delicious? M-m-m-m!

Four advantages your doctor sees in Cream of Wheat. It is digested rapidly . . . digestion starting right in the mouth. It is a factor in stimulating steady weight gains. It supplies protein for muscle-building. It gives quick food energy.

Economical? You bet! Two big helpings of Cream of Wheat for less than one cent. Each package cooks up to over 50 servings. It's the best hard wheat, too—sun-ripened in the finest growing areas. Heat-treated and blended to a special formula. 3½ million bowls are eaten daily!

Copr. 1937 by The Cream of Wheat Corporation

CREAM OF WHEAT

frigerators, Velveeta cheese, and a series for Pabst. His
first series of full-page color advertisements was for
Wyeth Laboratories, beginning in 1938.

Along with these jobs for advertising agencies,
Anderson continued receiving commissions for story
illustrations from the nation's top magazines. All three
Collier's magazines ran his pictures—*Woman's Home
Companion, Collier's, Redbook;* the Hearst publica-
tions, *Good Housekeeping* and *Cosmopolitan; Saturday
Evening Post* and *Ladies' Home Journal* in Philadelphia;
Today's Woman; McCalls. The authors for whom Harry
illustrated stories included Jesse Stuart, Faith Baldwin,
I. A. R. Wylie, Paul Gallico, Mary O'Hara (of *My Friend
Flicka* fame), and the Gilbreths who wrote *Cheaper by
the Dozen.*

The respective art directors of the magazines would
send him the stories they wanted illustrated and give him
an idea of the amount of space they could devote to the
picture. It was up to Harry to read the manuscript, become familiar with its punch and appeal, and come up
with a picture that would both get the casual reader into
the story and illuminate it for him.

By 1940 the magazines could afford four-color illustrations for their stories. Several authors wrote to Harry
to tell him they thought he did a better job telling their
story with his picture than they had done.

Like most illustrators, Harry works largely from
photographs. To hire a live model to pose for the several
hours or days necessary to complete a figure would be
prohibitively expensive. An hour's session with a camera
can produce a wide variety of poses from which to work.
Stevens-Gross paid the expenses for the model and
photographer, but it was usually up to the artist to find
the model to suit his need. Sometimes a model would be
hired from an agency; often he found people in his own
studio who served the purpose.

One day Harry arranged for a young woman from
another office in the same building to pose for a story

Anderson story illustrations were popular features in *Collier's,
Woman's Home Companion, Cosmopolitan, Good Housekeep-
ing, Saturday Evening Post, McCall's, Redbook,* and *Today's
Woman.* The one at left appeared in the early 1940's.

illustration in *Woman's Home Companion*. Ruth Huebel was receptionist for David Smart, publisher of *Esquire* magazine, whose office was on the thirty-sixth floor, Palmolive Building's penthouse. It was Ruth's first time to pose as a model; the next time she posed for Harry she was his wife, for they were married a year after they met.

Ruth's background was as different from Harry's as day is from night. Whereas he had two brothers and a sister, she was an only child. As a boy he had learned to make do or do without; in her home there had always been plenty of money. Yet he had known only strength and security in his home; hers had been an agonizing childhood.

When Ruth was 12 her parents separated permanently. At the age of 18 she married a man fourteen years her senior. A year later a son, Jared, was born. At this point

**Harry Anderson
and Ruth Huebel
shortly before
their marriage.**

her mother made her home with the young couple. She lived with Ruth for the rest of her life, some twenty-four years.

Ruth was married seven years to her first husband but as his work required constant traveling he spent a total of less than one year at home. They grew away from each other and finally were divorced. Ruth found a job with *Esquire*; her mother took care of young Jared.

Harry and Ruth's differences were just what each needed to balance their personalities. Ruth's entire life, childhood and marriage, had been but a string of broken promises. She desperately needed firm support, a man she could utterly depend on. Harry Anderson was that kind of man. And Harry, quiet and retiring, benefited from Ruth's spirited animation. They made an attractive couple, too, the tall young man with broad shoulders and shy grin and the brunette with a good eye for clothes design. Even on eighteen dollars a week and a family to support, Ruth had managed to look stylish.

A year or so after taking a family, Anderson took another step up the professional ladder—he joined Haddon Sundblom, a free-lance artist in the same building where Harry was working. One of Sundblom's accounts was Coca-Cola. Anderson's own reputation was well established now at *Good Housekeeping, Ladies' Home Journal, Saturday Evening Post,* et cetera, and he no longer needed contact men to make sales for him. He also designed billboard ads and full-page magazine ads for national corporations.

At the outbreak of World War II, Harry was a bit too old to be called; besides he had four dependents, for Tim was born to Ruth and Harry in October of 1941. A daughter, Kristin, came along in 1943. Even so, Harry was called to the Army near the end of the war, but the call was abruptly canceled. Two weeks later he was called again, but was told again not to come. Then the war ended.

But Anderson did make some contribution to the war effort—he was asked to "donate" posters. He designed a poster to curb idle talk, for which the Army gave him an official citation. It showed farm parents before a window in which hung a blue star, signifying they had a son in the service. But they were weeping over a government telegram crumpled in their hands. The caption read, "Ameri-

Anderson's first illustration for The Review and Herald Publishing Association, painted in 1944, was a black-and-white picture of nineteenth-century revivalist William Miller.

cans suffer when careless talk kills!"

Harry also visited the military hospitals in his area and made charcoal portraits free, to cheer up the soldiers and sailors recuperating there.

As the economy picked up in the early forties, Harry began getting more and more orders for illustrations. But with the increased business he began developing terrible cramps in his stomach. Doctors could not diagnose the trouble. He couldn't keep food down. For a year he lived on strained baby foods. Finally the problem was spotted—Harry Anderson was allergic to the turpentine in his oil paints. The only alternative was water-based paints. Harry's style of painting required opaque colors. Fortunately he had had experience in that medium since before he enrolled in the University of Illinois. So he substituted egg tempera for oils until the company that made it went out of business. After briefly trying acrylics, he used casein for many years.

32

Each time he switched to a new medium he ran into a new set of problems in technique. But part of Harry's strength is that he is firmly in charge of his art. He is not tied down to a certain medium or a certain style or a certain technique. He is always ahead of the game. As Sundblom once described him, "The difference between Anderson and other artists is that Anderson has knowledge."

Sometimes in his early days with Sundblom, Anderson would go to him for consultation on a painting problem. After Sundblom had told him how he would handle it, Anderson would leave, his brow knitted in concentration. When the job was finished it would be done Anderson's way.

It was about this time also that Harry developed what became known as his split-brush technique. When he needed to blend colors on a rounded surface such as a cylinder, Harry would take the handle end of his brush, dip it into some light-colored paint, and bang it down on his cardboard pallet. Then with the brush end he would pick up a load of dark color with half the bristles and the light paint with the other half. With this brush load and an amazingly long stroke, he produced the contours he needed, perhaps an arm or a silk-stockinged leg. The effect of the two colors mingling in his brush and on the canvas was like that of an airbrush, producing very smooth, graduated tones. It was especially effective on a face, arm, leg, or the fold of a garment.

Other artists tried to copy this method from Anderson, and some became captured by it, but none matched Anderson's skill. But for him it was not a gimmick. When he reached the place that he could produce the same effects in a better way he discarded the split brush.

After three or four years of living in rented quarters, Harry and Ruth went house buying. He was at the top of his profession; his family was growing; and he wanted a studio of his own. They found and purchased a beautiful home in Highland Park. Situated on a secluded lot on a main street just half a block from Lake Michigan, the three-story house had five bedrooms and two baths. It even had a butler's pantry. (It had been the home of the parents of James Aubrey, who later became president of a national radio network.) The previous owner already had some architectural plans drawn up for modernizing the front of the house, and Harry planned to turn the third floor into his studio. But Someone else had some other designs for Harry Anderson.

The purchase was finalized in late autumn. With winter coming on, the windows had to be washed, storm windows put up, and other odd jobs done incidental to taking over a "new" but used home. Harry didn't have the time to spare, so he arranged with an employment agency for a handyman to come out and do the work. Again, how strange that such small decisions can alter one's whole life.

John Stoller was the name of the man who came. Ruth was impressed from the start with the conscientiousness with which he did his work, as well as his cheerfulness and the manner of his speech. Instead of talking about himself, there was a certain seriousness and even spiritual aspect to his words. At noon Ruth urged John to join her and her mother for their usual hot lunch, where she began asking him questions regarding his beliefs.

After lunch John continued with his work, but Ruth Anderson plied him with so many more questions he was unable to finish that first day. In the evening when Harry came home, Ruth had much to tell him. The next evening she had even more. John Stoller, it was learned, was a Seventh-day Adventist. In addition to his unusual diet pattern he kept Saturday as Sabbath and seemed to have Bible support for his beliefs.

Ruth was sorry to see Stoller finish his work. She had many more questions.

"If you like, I can come over some evening," Stoller offered. "We can study the Bible together when your husband is present." Harry agreed with this proposal, so a regular weekly appointment was set up. Stoller drove fourteen or fifteen miles to their home after his day's work. He brought with him a small projector and film-strips that helped to make the study more interesting.

Harry Anderson had not had much contact with religion since childhood. His mother was a Lutheran, and

"What Happened to Your Hand?" is a favorite with parents and children the world over. Painted in 1945, to illustrate a series of children's books, this picture broke new ground in the field of graphic art by representing Christ in a contemporary setting.

Harry Anderson

he had attended a Congregational church as a boy, but even then he had puzzled over the discrepancy between the day of the week specified in the fourth commandment and the day observed by most Christians. Then he had dropped out of attending church except for an occasional visit to hear Norman Vincent Peale, pastor of the University church in Syracuse when Harry was in that city.

Point by point, as Stoller presented the tenets of his faith as taught in Scripture, the Andersons considered them. They were methodical in their study, yet their search was undergirded by a genuine love for Christ and an earnest desire to know His will in their lives. Harry Anderson had never been a bad man, but he had never before given first place to Jesus Christ. When he did, he gave it wholeheartedly, like he does everything.

Eventually, Ruth agreed to attend the church where Stoller worshiped, in Waukegan. But she was not prepared for what she found. Stoller's church group, numbering some thirty or forty people, was new and struggling and without a church home. They met in a mezzanine off the lobby of the Karcher Hotel. Ruth was embarrassed to be found in such a place, to be associated with such a "peculiar sect." She determined not to go again. But she forgot to tell Stoller. The next Saturday morning when he showed up at their home to accompany them to "his church," she didn't want to be rude so she agreed to go with him once more. This time the church met in a Masonic lodge. Some members had had to come early to sweep up cigarette butts and arrange the chairs, but from Ruth's viewpoint it was private at least.

Lifetime habits were harder for the Andersons to change than were theological concepts. Harry habitually smoked a pack or two of cigarettes a day. But when he learned that his body was intended to be a temple of the Holy Spirit he broke off his habit abruptly. Ruth had stopped smoking earlier, at Harry's urging—he didn't like to see women smoke, and it was easier for

Noah offers a sacrifice of thanksgiving as he, his family, and the animals that were with him in the ark debark safely after the Flood. The artist's composition and lighting tell the story powerfully here.

37

her to stop than to sneak a smoke when he wasn't around. But there were other problems. Her friends often served cocktails at social gatherings. When she was hostess and served lemonade, she felt they were offended.

At about this time John Stoller moved to another part of the State, but he turned over his interest in the Harry Andersons to Inez Morey, a Bible instructor. With her intuition into a woman's feelings, Inez was able to help Ruth to a right perspective on the attitude of one's friends as related to the will of one's supreme Friend.

Another crisis arose when Harry realized he could not in conscience continue to paint illustrations for beer advertisements and fiction stories. To Ruth this seemed to threaten their livelihood.

"What will we do?" she cried. "I don't want to give up my lovely home!" Again Inez helped her to put Christ first over her possessions. Harry and Ruth learned to see the way of the Christian life as the way of total love, not just a system of do's and don'ts. As Ruth likes to put it, they "found grace."

In March, 1943, daughter Kristin was born to Harry and Ruth Anderson. A month or two later the artist and his wife drove to Chicago's North Shore Seventh-day Adventist church and were baptized; their membership was duly inscribed in the Waukegan rolls. Immediately they joined with the other members in a building fund and in other church activities. Within two years Harry was elected superintendent of the Sabbath school. He has never felt at ease speaking in public, and the fact that he served in this capacity was evidence of the depth of his spiritual experience.

Harry's patience and even temperament were called to the test many times in his own home. His efforts to rear Jerry were often countered by Jerry's grandmother, who did not agree at all with Harry and Ruth's new faith. As might be expected, young Jerry learned to take advantage of this variance. Yet he also benefited from his stepfather's consistent discipline. Jerry always knew where the man stood on matters of morality and principle. Harry Anderson is not one who is beset with conflicts of ambivalence. Being very logical, he reasons problems through rather than succumbing to emotions.

He tried to establish a father-son relationship with Jerry. He took him fishing—even though Harry himself has never enjoyed taking any kind of life—and to base-ball games. He bought him an airplane-glider kit, which Jerry pursued for half an hour and then lost interest. Then, perhaps by way of object lesson, but also because of his own enthusiasm for working with his hands, Harry bought himself a model-airplane kit, a bi-wing Navy dive bomber. A balsa-wood-and-tissue-paper model, the kit required hours of painstaking cutting and gluing. Anderson was not satisfied with the plastic engine that was supplied, so he made his own out of metal. He even painted the individual rivet heads on the wing and fuselage surfaces.

As Jerry watched him work he mused, "I wish I could do that." Harry looked him in the eye and asked, "How bad do you wish it?" That question has served as a guide-post to Jerry ever since—if you want to do a thing bad enough, you can do it. Jerry is now a pilot for a national airline.

Harry's question is also a window into his own psyche, for he is the epitome of strict self-discipline. For example, he enjoys golf and has scored in the high 70's. With his powerful swing and strict self-control he would have made a top-notch pro. For that matter, such self-control would have made Harry Anderson a success at any career he chose.

In 1944 Anderson's pastor, Dr. Glenn Millard, asked him whether he would be willing to use his artistic talent for the Seventh-day Adventist Church. With a quiet "Yes," Anderson launched himself into a new phase of his profession.

Anderson's son, Tim, posed many times, in various costumes, for this fetching illustration of "The Gossamer World," a story by Faith Baldwin in *Collier's*.

PIONEERING
IN RELIGIOUS ART

The Seventh-day Adventist publishing program is one of the most extensive in the religious field. It produces textbooks, books for inspiration and on health, storybooks, periodicals on religious liberty, materials for youth and for Bible study. Much of the literature is for church consumption; a large share of it is sold to the public. More than fifty publishing houses around the world pour out this flood of material in several hundred languages.

The oldest and one of the largest of these houses, established even before the church itself was organized, is the Review and Herald Publishing Association. It is situated in Washington, D.C., just across the District boundary from a suburb called Takoma Park, and next door to the church's world headquarters. Management and editorial offices, periodical circulation, typesetting, printing, and binding are all under the roof of a three-story building.

At the time Terence ("T.K.") Martin joined the Review art department, it consisted of one artist-photographer and a file clerk. They had no time for the illustrating of large books, so the general manager assumed this responsibility. The only sources for religious pictures were old Bibles and books illustrated by nineteenth-century artists, such as Gustave Doré and Heinrich Hofmann.

"The Divine Healer." For this picture, painted in 1948, T. K. Martin, art director for the Review and Herald, posed as the father; Anderson's son, Tim, is the sick boy. Note the mixture of awe and wonder written on the face of the lad in the background.

42

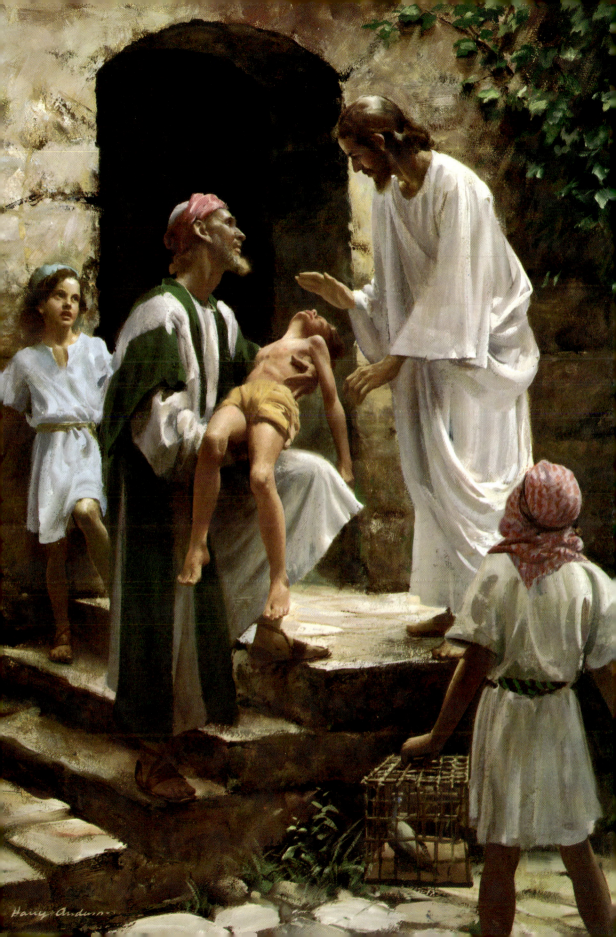

HARRY ANDERSON

These clipped reproductions were stored in a file. When a book was to be illustrated, the manager would go through the file, select the clippings of pictures to be used, and send them to an out-of-state artist who would have photo enlargements made of the clippings. The artist would work these over with opaque black and white water colors, making changes or adaptations as necessary. The result was something comparable to what is now considered a rough preliminary sketch. From these, however, photo-engravings were made for printing.

Later, two more artists were added to the staff of the Review. They worked on the top floor where, without air conditioning, perspiration ran down the artists' arms and spoiled their work—until fans were installed; then they had trouble keeping papers in order. The quartet shared one pair of scissors among them. But they made the most of their resources and cooperated in the production of some important books.

Martin realized the Review would have to be educated to grasp the place that real art could and should have in its publications. What then went under the name, he felt, was not worthy of the church's message. But then, some churchmen thought all pictures were a waste of space that could be put to better use in the text.

T. K.'s burden was not only for pictures that would help to tell the doctrines, but that readers should be able to identify with the pictures. Show Jesus in modern settings, illustrating the fact that He lives today. In a picture of the resurrection that attends Christ's second coming, let the people appear in the costumes of the respective periods in which they died, rather than everyone dressed in white.

When the book *Thoughts on Daniel and the Revelation,* by Uriah Smith, was scheduled for revision and re-printing, a joint operation with several other denominational publishing houses, the work of re-illustration fell to the Review. Martin felt that it was time to enlist the talents of some top-notch illustrators in addition to the artists on the Review staff. He secured the services of

"The First Sabbath." A vesper mood settles upon Adam and Eve and the Garden of Eden. Landscape painting is one of Harry Anderson's favorite subjects.

Franklin Booth and Frederick Gruger, both of whom had illustrated for *The Saturday Evening Post.* They turned out excellent pictures illustrating the three angels of Revelation 14 and the king's dream of Daniel 2, as well as of the second coming of Jesus and other subjects. But while they worked successfully in black and white, they were not strong with the use of color. Sensing the trend toward more use of color in book illustration, Martin anticipated the day when the Review might develop an illustrator expert in color work.

One day Laura Clement, editor of *The Youth's Instructor,* came down the hall with a sheaf of magazine pages in her hand. "Brother Martin, would you please look at this. Dr. Millard, pastor of the Waukegan church, sent these—he wants to know whether you can use this artist's work in the *Instructor.*"

T. K. recognized the work immediately. He had been keeping a file of clippings of Harry Anderson's work. In addition to the artist's sense of composition and tonal values, Martin was particularly impressed with his mastery of lights and shadows. They reproduced well, whether in black and white or in color.

"This man is now a Seventh-day Adventist," Miss Clement went on. "He wants to serve the church."

Martin was electrified. He didn't walk down the long hallway to the office of the general manager, W. P. Elliott— he ran. "This is the quality of work this house needs," Martin cried. "Harry Anderson is one of the top illustrators. I would like to write him and invite him to come and work for the Review."

"Don't write him," Elliott countered. "Telephone him." In twenty years Martin had never been authorized to make a long-distance telephone call, but it was well for the Review that he was now, for it developed that one of the other denominational houses was also trying to sign up Harry Anderson.

Even so, six weeks passed before Anderson was able to get away from Chicago long enough to come to Washing-

© REVIEW AND HERALD

This painting, done in 1949, is one of Anderson's early attempts to portray the joys of the new earth, after sin has been eradicated, as described in Isaiah and Revelation.

47

ton to look over the situation and discuss whether he could move there to work. Martin met the train at a suburban station near the Review. Car after car was empty. Finally he came to the last car and met a man in a raincoat with his collar turned up, shoulders hunched. "Would you be Harry Anderson?" It was.

A long talk with Martin and Elliott impressed Harry with the need of the Review and Herald for his talents. He returned to Chicago with the appeal, but his wife turned down the idea for the time being. Denominational pay was scaled considerably lower than equivalent work "outside." There was not even a pay scale category for professionally skilled artists of Harry Anderson's caliber. The Andersons would not be able to maintain their standard of living, and besides, Ruth loved her Highland Park home.

Harry was willing, however, to do some free-lance work for the Review. His first few pictures illustrated early denominational history and were in black and white. The Review could not afford to purchase many color pictures and reproduce them in color. But Harry had a suggestion. "I would as soon do the pictures in color—it is easier for me, and I won't charge you any more." Well, no one could turn down an offer like that.

But Harry's first picture in color provoked a crisis—and proved to be a turning point in Seventh-day Adventist art. Martin asked for a picture to illustrate a story in *The Children's Hour,* by "Uncle Arthur" Maxwell. The story was of a mother whose hands were scarred and ugly. Her daughter was ashamed of the appearance of her mother's hands until she learned that they had been scarred in saving her, as a baby, from a fire. Then to the girl they were the most beautiful hands in the world. Harry was to paint a picture of Christ in His traditional white robes, talking to children in modern, contemporary dress, in a garden. A little girl on Jesus' lap would be asking Him to tell about the scar prints in His hands.

This was Anderson's first attempt to portray the figure of Christ. He used as a model another artist in his studio,

Jesus referred to the angel that cares for each girl and boy (Matt. 18:10). Here the artist pictures an angel guarding his charge while she trustingly sleeps.

T. K. Martin discusses some fine points with Anderson.

Gene Modesett, who had the clear-cut features that Anderson felt Christ would have. The expression on Jesus' face came from Harry's own experience with a loving Saviour. So determined was he to get the right expression that he washed out the head six times. The seventh attempt was successful.

For the finished picture, titled "What Happened to Your Hand?" the Review paid Harry two hundred dollars, the most they had paid anyone, but still only a fraction of what Harry was getting from his commercial work. The difference in price was his contribution to the cause he had espoused.

In a scene from Seventh-day Adventist Church history, Anderson pictures James White and his wife, Ellen, kneeling, with friends, around the first issues of early church publications before they are mailed out to readers.

**The artist
and his young son, Tim.**

Publication of "What Happened to Your Hand?" created considerable criticism. One of T. K. Martin's stoutest friends claimed it was incongruous to portray Jesus in traditional clothes in the same picture with children in modern dress. Even a General Conference official objected to the concept.

Martin and his assistant art director were sent to a convention of sales personnel in Grand Rapids, Michigan, where Martin was invited to explain how the house was trying to update its art, not only in quality but in concept. He detailed how they were developing a line of original pictures tailor-made for the church's message in Bible doctrines and prophecies. They were an attempt to por-

The promise of a Redeemer is made to Adam and Eve. This early picture was first painted in black and white.

tray an ever-present Christ who is the same yesterday, to-day, and forever, who is "with us in our homes, in our offices, on the playground."

Some of those present at the meeting were not quite sure of this new approach in art, especially as exemplified in "What Happened to Your Hand?" Others were enthusi-astic. As these were the people responsible for selling the books Anderson's pictures appeared in, their opinion was crucial.

Then T. K.'s assistant spoke up, surprising even Martin with his words. "I opposed this picture when I first saw it," he said. "I felt it was incongruous, almost unethical. But my little girl was sitting on the floor one evening, look-ing at her copy of *The Children's Hour.* She came to this picture and was entranced by it. Then she came over and said to me, 'Daddy, I want to sit on Jesus' lap too.' It broke me up. I approve of these pictures, now."

That statement settled the matter as far as that con-vention was concerned, and the small girl's reaction, multiplied a hundred thousand fold, vindicated the con-cept in general. "What Happened to Your Hand?" became world famous and today is probably Anderson's best-known work.

(Left) Anderson has painted several pictures of the resurrection of the just; this was his first. He remains unsatisfied with any of his attempts to portray the Second Coming. The event, he feels, will surpass in glory and trauma any human effort to describe. (Overleaf, left) The game of life, a battle in the great controversy between Christ and Satan. Man's eternal destiny is at stake. (Overleaf, right) A contemporary version of the parable of the prodigal son.

THE ARTIST
AT WORK

The Review and Herald Publishing Association manager, W. P. Elliott, made another personal appeal to Harry and Ruth, and in 1946 they at last agreed to move to the Washington area. Harry would work for the Review as a free-lance artist, supplementing the work they could give him by accepting assignments from national magazines.

The Review agreed to sell the Andersons a large frame house and thirteen acres of land on Ray Road, a couple of miles away. On a preliminary visit Ruth looked the house over. A previous owner had been embalmed in the bathtub—a brown stain marred the bottom and for a distance of six or eight inches up the inside walls. Because of the war, there was a shortage of building materials in Washington, so Ruth arranged for a new tub as well as new wallpaper to be sent from Chicago. But when the tub arrived, it was found to face the wrong direction and had to be exchanged, and the wallpaper hanger insisted on being paid the profit he had lost by not supplying the paper. Harry took all this with equanimity.

For a studio for Harry, the Review made available the front bedroom on the second floor of a house a block from the publishing establishment. It did not have a proper north light, but it was better than the set-up on the third floor of the Review and was more private. But Anderson was not long alone. Vernon Nye, who had been doing pen and ink drawings on salary for the Review, was interested in illustrating with brush and paint. He asked for the opportunity to work with the nationally known artist.

Harry Anderson is scared off by the word "teacher."

58

A picture of the artist standing at his easel appeared in the
(Washington) *Sunday Star*.

59

A man of few remarks, he finds it difficult to convey information by words. If asked a direct question he answers it straightforwardly. Occasionally he would demonstrate with a brush mark or two on Nye's illustration board. He knew many famous artists personally, but he never indulged in "name-dropping" or discussing their techniques. Yet Anderson had—and has—strong feelings on certain aspects of painting.

"Conception, composition, values, colors, drawing, and painting dexterity," says Harry, "must all work together. And they are important in just that order. The younger artist is likely to forget one or the other. But the parts all become automatic, in time."

His tonal values, along with his handling of details, are probably what other artists notice first in Harry's work. Tonal values in art refer to the balance of light and dark (regardless of color) as they are used on the different objects within a composition. The proper use of these values in relation to the light source brings out the *form* of an object, making it three dimensional on a flat page.

In viewing a scene, the human eye is able to focus on only one area or plane at a time; all the rest is out of focus. The artist may try to duplicate this effect in a painting by drawing out of focus, or only sketching, unimportant surroundings and concentrate interest on the focal point of the picture by increased contrast, attention to detail, pure color, and various other devices.

From a distance Anderson's work looks as though it were done in great detail. Up close it looks as though it were done casually. In point of fact, neither assessment is true. Harry has a way, through carefully drawn strokes, of only suggesting detail. He feels the beholder enjoys a picture more when he himself interprets what has been suggested by the artist.

Anderson may spend hours to get the right effect of looseness. After working all day on a head the size of a half dollar, he may scrub it all out and start afresh. On the other hand, he is not intimidated by his own craft. One

Mother and daughter, Ruth and Kristin Anderson, posed for a story illustration in *Collier's* magazine.

day T. K. Martin suggested that a high light in an illustration was a trifle strong and attracted too much attention to itself. Anderson, though he may not have agreed, was willing to accommodate Martin. He licked his thumb and dulled the offending high light. "Is that better?" he asked. Martin happily accepted it.

As Michelangelo once observed, "Trifles make perfect, but perfection is no trifle."

The photographs Anderson works from need not be in color; in fact, most of them he takes and develops himself. Next to Harry's studio a second bedroom was fixed up for a photo studio and darkroom. (He also set up a ping-pong table in there.) He selected models from among his friends or scoured the neighborhood for them. To pay them by the hour while he painted would be prohibitively expensive—a professional model may command as much as sixty dollars an hour. But by posing his models in approximately the right costume and photographing them, Harry could obtain what he needed—the proper foreshortening of limbs, inclination of head, relationship of light and shadow.

Then the artist would compose the picture, perhaps combining elements from several photos. A Western scene, for instance, might make use of three pictures—a man on horseback, timber detail, and a distant mountain skyline. The artist must get his values right, have the angle of light consistent, make sure the details are authentic in every respect, and get the proper expression on the faces of his figures.

Never one for ostentation, Harry Anderson would fit in with most people's idea of an ordinary farmer. Wearing a flannel shirt and plaid cap, he drove around Takoma Park in a jeep to get back and forth to work or to look for models for his illustrations. He worked in the same clothes.

Some artists would be bothered by Anderson's work habits. When he did a self-portrait to accompany an article written about him in *American Artist* (May, 1956),

Above the din of the busy city that teems with humanity representing all strata of society, the Creator and Redeemer looks after His own. To each person He still gives the invitation, "Come unto me, all ye that labour and are heavy laden."

The Anderson residence on Ray Road. Harry built a
studio behind the house.

In the book of Revelation, a series of startling and profound
messages is prophesied for earth's latter days, each to be deliv-
ered "with a loud voice" by a flying angel. Here is Anderson's
rendition of the scene.

he hung a sheet across the studio wall behind him to hide the clutter. His paintings may be likened to a beautiful water lily that grows from the bottom of a pond.

On any given picture Anderson first does a lot of research—it is not unusual for him to spend more time in preparation than in the actual painting. He even cut his own leather thongs for a model of how they would drape on Christ's sandals. If his assignment is a Bible picture he will study Bible encyclopedias. If his job is to paint a series of vintage cars, he goes through old *National Geographics.* This work is for the background, as well as for detail about costume and other pertinent features.

Then an observer would see Harry studying the floor for half a day, his face in a scowl, as he thinks out the picture. He makes a dozen or more doodles until he has a fair idea of the best composition.

When he gets ready to work he kicks papers aside, clearing a place for himself before his easel. Unlike most artists, he stands at his work. At one time he wore a white apron with bib over his clothes, but later he left that off in favor of comfortable old clothes. Painting can be dirty work, and his clothes—and sometimes the woodwork—show it.

Anderson likes to start each new job with a brand-new brush. But he doesn't throw away the old brushes. So in his studio stand jars, vases, and bowls stuffed with dozens of old brushes. To clean his brush between colors he dips it into a large bowl of water. (Those who observe him say he apparently never changes the water; after a while it gets to be like soup, but he seems to prefer it that way.)

From his doodles Harry will make one or two sketches in casein to check out his composition and to make sure of color balance. He lays off the sketch in squares with black thread to facilitate reproduction. Then he starts drawing, in paint, directly onto his working canvas. He does not sketch in pencil or charcoal on his canvas.

As he works, in his left hand he holds the photo from

HARRY ANDERSON

which he is working at the moment, or a magnifying glass, or a mall stick, a support for his drawing hand when working in details. His face screws up in concentration and his left foot finds its way to rest on top of his right foot. Occasionally he wipes his brush on his pants to clean it or to remove excess paint.

Some artists, under the strain of concentration—and perhaps more than a bit of egotism—become almost unbearable when working. The story is told that Goya, when painting the Duke of Wellington's portrait, became exasperated at his subject and threw a handful of paint brushes at him. Although Harry concentrates heavily on his work, to the point he is almost out of touch with his surroundings, he does not become exasperated like that.

When the Andersons first arrived in Takoma Park, Elliott and Martin introduced them to professional people in the area. With Ronald Senseman (architect), George Groome (chemist), Wayne MacFarland (physician), and their wives, the Andersons could let down their hair. Harry enjoyed playing his guitar with them or a game of Scrabble.

Gib Crockett, nationally syndicated cartoonist on the *Washington Star* newspaper, met Harry on an assignment. After that he often stopped by with the intention of watching Harry work, hoping to pick up some hints that would help him in his own art. Harry drew him instead to the ping-pong table or to the horseshoe pit outside. Gib at least had the satisfaction that he could beat Harry pitching horseshoes.

One day Anderson invited Crockett to set up an easel in the studio with him. "Harry," the cartoonist warned, "if I move in here I'll steal everything you've got." Crockett was referring to Harry's professional techniques, but the latter, who is as full of generosity as he is short of guile, mulled over the words a minute and then replied quietly, "Well, I'll go and buy some more."

Happily, Harry Anderson the artist and T. K. Martin the art director found in each other kindred spirits. Theirs

The painting at right can be interpreted both literally and figuratively: Christ's care for His own extends to their travels on land, at sea, and in the air; also, He is an infallible Guide on the journey of life.

Harry loves to help things grow.
He has had a garden at each
home he has owned.

(Left) To Adam were brought all the newly created animals to be named. Although painting animals is not his specialty, Anderson did a remarkable job on a difficult assignment.

(Overleaf) Again placing Jesus in a contemporary setting, Anderson shows Him illustrating, by the action of the wind on trees and flowers, to a modern Nicodemus the invisible effects of the Holy Spirit on the human life.

71

HARRY ANDERSON

was a case of instant compatibility; they recognized in each other the marks of a true gentleman. Harry says, with characteristic magnanimity, "Terence Martin deserves the credit for most of my success as a religious artist. He is an idea man."

Martin returns the compliment: "Harry is a complete master of lights and shadows, of forms, of the values of colors. He goes beyond the photograph; he is able to put himself into his pictures, so it is important that his own personality be good."

As an art director for religious paintings, Martin championed the cause of propriety, especially in the portrayal of Jesus Christ. Christ should always be presented with the height of respect, the focal point of any picture. His features and actions should always reveal the nobility and dignity of His personality. Even in a simple design, His face should be free from distortion or caricature. And Martin found Harry in complete agreement with this ideal.

As a comparatively new Adventist, however, Anderson did not always catch just the nuance that Martin had in mind for his pictures. One assignment, for instance, was for a painting of Jesus appealing to the United Nations. The picture, to be a cover for the religious journal *Liberty,* was to show Jesus in traditional robe knocking at the Secretariat building even as He is often portrayed knocking at the heart's door. Anderson made a trip to New York City and photographed the building. In his picture he showed a clear, blue sky—Harry feels that ordinarily the sky should be unobtrusive, that a common mistake among artists is to overpower their pictures by drawing too much attention to it. But in this case Martin had a counter suggestion. The background mood of the picture was to be one of gloom, emphasizing Jesus Christ as the true Hope of the nations. The art director asked Harry to paint a threatening sky, representing angry nations. This, too, became a famous picture.

Similarly, from time to time Martin had Harry remove a boy's cap in the Saviour's presence, or put a businessman in a forward-leaning, expectant posture as he listened to Jesus' words, rather than to lean back in a self-confident air. On his part, Harry agreed with and appreciated these pointers. As Vernon Nye says, while Anderson recognizes the buyer's right to order what he

74

wants, when it comes to technique Anderson has complete confidence in what he is doing. "He knows his craft backwards and forwards and upside-down."

To augment his income from pictures for the Review and Herald, every month or six weeks Harry painted a picture for a national magazine. Whereas the Review paid him two hundred dollars or so for a picture, he could get much more from the *Ladies' Home Journal, Woman's Home Companion,* or *McCall's.* These jobs were critical to his livelihood, for as a free-lance artist he received none of the "fringe benefits" enjoyed by regular Review employees, such as medical and educational allowances, vacation with pay, or retirement fund.

(Overleaf, left) Moses receives the Ten Commandments, written by God's own finger on stone tablets.
(Overleaf, right) Jesus, the Friend of children everywhere.

75

HARRY ANDERSON

One important job Harry executed was a year's worth of covers for *Woman's Home Companion.* Brother-and-sister situations were the theme; he used the same two models throughout, Peggy Senseman and his own son Tim, a little younger. He painted them in scenes appropriate to the season of the year that each respective cover was to be used—playing in the snow, examining a starfish on the beach. In one scene Peggy was dropping cherries into her "brother's" mouth.

Tim quickly developed into a top-notch model for his dad. He could put on just the expression the job called for. In a story illustration he posed as a sick boy. The woebegone look on his face could tug at anybody's heartstrings. Tim's own favorite picture illustrated a story by Faith Baldwin in which the boy hero imagined himself in many daring roles. The picture showed Tim stretched out on the grass, thoroughly enjoying little miniatures of himself as a train engineer, a doctor, farmer, big-game hunter, as a Martian, even as a cowboy riding a grasshopper. Perhaps his enjoyment of the role as artist's model is one reason Tim took up drama in college.

Tim's sister Kristin posed for many pictures too, as did her mother and even Harry Anderson himself. In one picture Harry appeared no less than five times, but only someone with prior knowledge would notice it. It certainly cost less than to hire a professional. But Harry did not stint on expense if it was required to put out a first-rate job.

After a couple of years in the bedroom-cum-studio near the Review, Harry built his own studio just back of his home. Designed by his architect friend Senseman, the building was made of cinder block and measured some thirty by forty feet. It had a proper window and, inside, a balcony from which the artist could photograph his subject when the illustration required a high viewing angle.

At one end of the studio Harry built a workshop. His hands have to keep busy—painting is only one outlet for them. He had been a model maker from boyhood. Now

In a lesson drawn from the worship service of ancient Israel, the book of Hebrews dwells at some length on Christ's present role in heaven as the Christian's High Priest, his Mediator with the Father.

78

JANUARY 1949 25 CENTS

Woman's Home COMPANION ★

Breath-taking—**REMEMBER EVERY WORD**—*a new mystery by Helen Reilly*

DOGS AND CHILDREN NOT WANTED—*by Howard Whitman*

with his own workshop he was not limited to kits. He fashioned small models from scratch. He enjoys working with wood. From the knotty pine of an old barn on his Ray Road place, Harry fashioned a beautiful hutch cabinet. In both cabinetry and finish it was a first-class job.

Reared as a city boy, when Harry got some land under his feet he went in for gardening in a big way. A handyman plowed it up for him with a one-eyed horse, and Harry took over from there. He prepared the soil, laid off the rows, and cultivated the crops by hand. The growing of fruits and vegetables is another expression of his love for life. Ruth canned and froze the produce the family could not consume.

One day friends from the Waukegan church dropped in on the Andersons. Arthur and Ruby Rice were on their way to Florida. After a pleasant day or two reminiscing, as Rice prepared to continue his journey, Harry spoke to him. "Arthur, I could say, 'It was nice having you and do come again sometime,' but we're having a good time together. We have a big place here, and you can work here as well as in Florida. Why not stay with us awhile?"

In accepting that invitation Rice triggered a new but short-lived chapter in the Anderson chronicles. "Harry," he opened one day, "with all this land, why not make it pay for itself?"

"What do you have in mind?" Harry countered.

"You could raise chickens. They aren't much work. You just keep feed and water in front of them and after a few months collect your profit."

That sounded reasonable to Anderson. Rice remodeled some old buildings on the place as chicken dormitories, and Anderson bought two hundred baby roosters. Truly, they weren't much work—at first. After Arthur and Ruby had been with the Andersons about three months they went on to Florida. Just before leaving, Arthur filled Harry in on some of the facts of life.

"Those chicks are about six weeks old now. You should caponize them and they will flesh out better—get

For a year's supply of covers for *Woman's Home Companion*, Anderson painted his son, Tim, and a friend in a series of "brother and sister" situations.

a better price on the market."

"Caponize them?"

"Yes. It's like castrating a calf. The county agricultural agent can show you how."

The agent duly came over and proceeded to show Harry Anderson the art of caponizing chickens. It is a surgical operation, without, of course, the benefit of anesthesia for the patient. The first five birds the agent worked on died under his knife. "Well, anyway," he said to Harry, "you know how now," and he left. By the time Harry had finished the other 195 roosters, the entire idea of chicken farming had become extremely distasteful to him.

But the end was not yet. With their sex drives eliminated, the birds devoted themselves wholeheartedly to eating. Harry and Ruth were ready to agree that there *was* a lot of money in chicken-raising—*their* money. When the birds were ready for market it fell to Ruth to dress them. She fully agreed with Harry—no more chicken business.

At left is an example of the type of preliminary sketch Harry Anderson makes for his paintings. Note the improvements in composition in the finished picture on pages 104 and 105.

83

NEW ENGLAND
HOME

Six or seven years in the Takoma Park-Washington, D.C., area convinced Harry that it was not the place for him. For one thing, there was a dearth of good models. An artist's model must be adaptive, flexible, as well as graceful, natural, and unself-conscious. This usually takes training and certainly experience. Much of Harry's time was spent scouring the streets for the right figure—who would, of course, be an amateur—then coaching, posing, shooting, and re-shooting. Where a model agency is available he could simply call on the telephone and order an experienced model of a certain type, along with any studio props he might need.

Harry Anderson also needed to be among his peers. He needed the stimulation of companionship with others of his profession. Just as a tennis player or a golfer needs to play against someone of equal or better talent, Harry needed the criticism and the camaraderie of other top artists. If he stayed in Washington, without this continued contact, he could slip backward in his profession.

One day Anderson was on the telephone to the art director of *Woman's Home Companion* in New York City. There happened to be in the *Companion* office that day Harry's old sidekick from Syracuse, Tom Lovell. Tom was a successful artist living in southern New Eng-

Many poems have been written representing life as a stormy ocean passage. The artist portrays Christ as the Pilot who can safely see us through any storm. This painting is one of Ruth Anderson's favorites.

**The Anderson home
in New England. Note the black band around the
chimney, dating the house back to Revolutionary times.**

land. He enjoyed the pleasures of country life, yet he
was still conveniently near New York's art offices and
model agencies. The idea intrigued Anderson, and he accepted Tom's invitation to come up and visit.

Lovell took Harry house hunting. They found one a
short drive from the coast, situated on a five-acre lot on a
paved but little-used road about two miles from the
center of a town of five thousand population. Harry liked
the place and when Ruth saw it she agreed. They purchased it and moved in August, 1951.

The house is a genuine antique but kept in good repair. Built in the 1700's, it still has a black band around its
chimney top. This was a sign to the British, when they
were burning houses of rebels in the area, that a Tory
sympathizer lived there. The house rests on a fieldstone
foundation nearly two feet thick. Hewn timbers support

86

**Interior view
of the Anderson home.**

foot-wide floor boards. The original part of the house is
two stories high, with an attic that has been finished
with bedroom and bath. One-story additions have been
made on three sides. Low ceilings and a four-foot fireplace characterize the interior.

A springhouse stands behind the kitchen. A hundred
yards farther a root cellar, made of stone, burrows into the
hillside. A stone-lined compost pit is also nearby. In one
corner of the property is a small cottage just right for
Ruth's mother, who was still living with them when they
bought the property. Here she could have privacy yet be
close by. (Now daughter Kristin, married and with a
family, lives there. She is supervisor of a psychiatric
ward.)

On the other side of the main house is a tennis court
that hasn't seen a ball in many a year. Harry turned it

Harry Anderson painted the above picture of himself at work at the request of *American Artist* magazine to accompany an article that featured him in 1956.

into his garden area—the ten-foot chain-link fence seemed just the thing to keep deer out of his lettuce beds. But even though the fence goes into the ground several inches it cannot keep out coons and other animals that dig under or climb over. Yew bushes outline the yard, and large spruce trees frame the house. Giant marigolds splash against a low wall.

The studio is behind the house over a double garage. English ivy, growing up over the clapboard sides and

(Left) This representation of Mary and Baby Jesus was painted in 1956 to illustrate a volume of *The Bible Story,* a series of children's books.

onto the cedar shake roof, seems to be trying to blend it into the landscape. Harry started to paint it at one time, but the work took too much time from his art, so he stopped, half done.

The studio is without doubt a man's room, and a working man at that. Old gardening and paint clothes are thrown over an overstuffed chair. Garden tools take up one corner and woodworking tools another. At one time the high-ceilinged studio must have depended on a fireplace for heat; later an old Franklin stove with ornate chrome work was installed. But Anderson doesn't depend on fireplace or stove. He needs plenty of warmth as he works, so an oil-burning furnace supplies hot air. With such a high ceiling, the fuel bill is considerable.

On the balcony, along one wall of the studio, a small cot for cat naps shares space with yellow pine boards that are drying for some future cabinetry project. Under the balcony, Harry stores his *National Geographics* and an array of art books he picked up years ago in Chicago. These, and especially his drawers of art files, come in handy in his research.

The studio is on the upper level of a converted stable.

90

On the wall above an old desk that is loaded with papers, correspondence, old photos, and recent sketches, hangs Harry's "moose head." Actually, it is the stump of an old pear tree dug up from the yard, but its particular shape, with roots spreading out in the right proportions, does closely resemble a hunter's trophy.

Above the large window on the north side hangs a bank of fluorescent lights that can be adjusted in height. Below the window are racks of sewing thread in a rainbow of colors, and a sewing machine. Anderson sews many of the costumes needed for his pictures. He also mends his own clothes and those of the rest of the family, and stitches other items for the home. Ruth can't bear to sew; Harry loves it.

In the middle of all the clutter is Harry's easel. An imposing thing, it is supported by a heavy cast-iron stand. Harry has used the same easel for twenty-five or thirty years. Several cabinets of various sizes stand nearby, holding bent and spent paint tubes, rags, and brushes. Brushes are everywhere, perhaps six or eight dozen of them. A pad of palette paper completes the

**The artist's work area
for painting, carving, building, sewing.**

An artist paints an artist. For a series of advertisements for John Hancock Mutual Life Insurance Company, Anderson portrayed Winslow Homer, noted painter of ships and seas.

equipment, except for a small projector and improvised screen that the artist sometimes uses when the picture he is working from is a color slide.

Harry begins his day at the easel at about eleven o'clock each morning. Before that he may have worked in the garden or driven to town. It seems there's always something he needs from the hardware or photo shop, and Ruth usually has some need from the market. The small shopping district has retained its other-century flavor, and is itself one of the reasons the Andersons like the area. Also, there are many other artists—and writers—nearby.

Anderson paints until one-thirty or two o'clock, when Ruth will have a bowl of hot soup for him. He goes back to the studio until six, when dinner is served. For informal meals the family eats in the kitchen. After dinner dad returns to the studio to work until eleven o'clock or midnight. Sometimes, when the creative urge is on him, he will work until two or three o'clock in the morning.

Harry Anderson's creativity is so large it flows out in many forms. Besides painting he also sculps and carves, makes models and furniture. On a shelf in his studio is a clock he built—the gears are of rosewood and teak. In a corner is a large picture frame made of an ancient wooden house gutter. He "turned it inside out," cutting it so that the concave surface curves neatly away from the painting, setting it off to advantage.

The house is full of Harry's *objets d'art.* In the dining room, in addition to the handsome hutch that he made, is a bench fashioned after an old buggy seat. The living room features a lamp table created from a discarded drawing easel, and a sizable Shaker storage box that is dovetailed and glued, without a nail or screw in it. A vanity in an upstairs bedroom and a chest in the master bedroom further attest to the artist's skill in working with wood. A table, fashioned after an old tavern table, has been mistaken as a genuine antique even by dealers.

In one of the bedrooms stands a Shaker chest of drawers more than five feet tall. A miniature of it, built for his granddaughter, Gabrielle, graces the living room. Ruth loves Shaker furniture, and a number of Harry's creations reflect her interest. The pine boards drying in his studio are for a Shaker "settle," or bench seat.

93

Harry does not disdain to create with needle and thread. On the floor are eight or ten rugs of various motifs that he designed and hooked. He stitched the drapes at the dining room window, as well as his wife's blouse. He made the cushion on a chair. The headboard in the guest bedroom consists of an old picture frame he enhanced by adding a panel of patterned and quilted bed sheet.

Aside from the creative urge itself, Anderson enjoys the feel of wood in his hands. The floors and window sills of his home are adorned with two dozen or more carved birds. Mostly waterfowl, each is of a different species. A flock of ducks and a Canada goose "swim" in one corner; sandpipers, turnstones, and plovers, each standing on a single leg, vie for space on mantel and tabletop. An owl blinks from the cornice of a book chest. On the piano a guilded eagle stretches his pinions. Harry intended to mount the eagle on a weathervane on the roof, but Ruth could not bear to relegate such a magnificent work of art to the elements.

Standing guard beside the eagle is the wooden figure

of a country sheriff with gun in hand. The expression of his eyes seems to betoken a fear that he has taken on a job bigger than he is. Then there is a pair of wooden figures, an Amish farmer and his wife. She is holding a tiny basket over her arm—Harry wove the basket, too. This pair is so lifelike in stance and expression that in the perspective of a photograph they positively look alike. A model train, not unlike the Toonerville Trolley, was created from turpentine cans.

A black-and-red model of a one-horse buggy almost begs to be picked up and examined. Anderson fashioned the curved shafts by steaming the wood; the metal frames for the collapsible top he painstakingly made out of wire; the top itself and seat cushion display tiny little stitches. Each wooden wheel is rimmed authentically with a metal tire. The model makes one wish he were small enough to climb aboard for a jaunt into the past.

But the *pièce d'résistance* is a three-foot model clipper ship that rests in splendor on the dining room table. It is the three-masted schooner *Sovereign of the Seas,* and took Harry two years to build. A few metal items he purchased from a hobby store, but the rest was crafted with only a blueprint to aid him. The masts had been paintbrushes in his studio. The decking was laid down board by board, each only an eighth of an inch wide —he obtained them by shaving the edges of the wooden

slats from an old set of Venetian blinds. The rigging alone, or for that matter just the shrouds, which are woven of individual strands of thread, would more than tax the usual modelmaker. Harry loves a challenge.

Most of Harry Anderson's handicrafts were made as Christmas or birthday presents for his wife. He snatches

fifteen minutes here and there, as relief from his painting. Much can be accomplished in such odd moments, when they are concentrated toward a particular goal.

Although Ruth doesn't like sewing, she enjoys needlepoint and has turned out many excellent pieces. One, a favorite quotation framed in flowers (Harry worked out the design for her), was used as a four-color cover for *The Review and Herald*, the general church paper of the Seventh-day Adventist Church.

"The Prince of Peace." To the representatives of a troubled world Christ presents Himself as the only Source of real, enduring peace.

HARRY ANDERSON

Where Ruth really shines, however, is in her cooking. As Harry says, "She cooks with love." Homemade soups are her specialty, but she enjoys all aspects of the culinary art. The Andersons are health-oriented, and self-styled label-readers. Chemical additives and high-cholesterol items, even ready-made foods, are taboo in her kitchen. Harry is satisfied with simple foods, such as dried lima beans, lentils, peas, cooked in a variety of ways. Ruth splurges on fruit and delights in making attractive salads.

Her skill at homemaking is in quiet evidence throughout her home. In keeping with the house itself, she collects antiques. A copper bedwarmer and brass spoons glow by the fireplace. Dozens of pieces of milk china and cut glass find a place among the many live plants she keeps in the living room. Ancient clocks on mantel and wall and antique candleholders and snuffers contribute to the atmosphere.

One feature of the Anderson home, while it fosters the lived-in feeling, stems more from Harry's profession than from any choice of Ruth's. That is the sizable collection of hats and other paraphernalia that hang all about the house. Top hat, bowler, boater, other straw hats, helmet, visored caps of various designs, soldier's cap, miner's hard hat, a Cossack's fur hat—at some time Harry has needed each item as a prop for a picture, and Ruth doesn't feel free to throw anything away, for she never knows when he may need it again. A tennis racket without strings (Harry can paint them in), a riding crop, an old gun that doesn't shoot; housecleaning can be quite a chore.

Ruth naturally takes a personal interest in Harry's painting. She rarely visits him while he is at the easel—he can't concentrate when someone is watching—but she can tell from his spirit when the work is going well or if he is having problems. She recognizes her greatest contribution is in providing a well-run home and a loving atmosphere that leaves him free to do his best. She often

In His Sermon on the Mount, Christ emphasized the spirit of love that pervades His law, as opposed to a legalistic approach. Many viewers feel that in this face of Christ, Anderson has done his best work of portraying the strength, pity, and love of man's Redeemer.

prays for his hands and eyes, especially when he is doing a picture of Christ. Occasionally she does look in on his work and offers an opinion, a fresh perspective. Sometimes she may suggest that he has done enough on a picture and that to do more would spoil it.

The kind of painting Harry Anderson does is more hard work than glamour for him. When a visitor, even an old painter friend, drops in and starts to talk shop, Harry gently changes the conversation. "It's enough to do the work," he says; "why talk about it?"

There are two phases of the work that Harry enjoys—the beginning and the end. He likes the challenge of thinking out a picture, of composing it, first in his mind and then on paper. He likes to work out the problems of lighting, pose, and story-telling. And he enjoys putting on the finishing touches. It is often in those last ten or dozen strokes that he can really feel his picture is saying what he wants it to say.

Budding young artists occasionally ask Anderson, "How did you get to be famous?" Harry's reply is that he didn't start out with the ambition to become famous. "I've always tried to do my best. In my paintings I am giving of myself. It all boils down to simple, hard work." He doesn't lay claim to "inspiration" for his work, not "if you mean the light-bulb-turning-on, thunderbolt-from-the-sky, type of inspiration. It is simply concentrating on my job, applying the principles of art as I know them, and keeping on until the job is finished."

Usually this is translated as standing for long hours, eyes focused on a small area of canvas, painting in, washing off, and painting in again. Ruth frequently seeks to relieve the tedium and tension by providing him with diversions in the form of a garment to mend, a broken chair to repair, or some project to build. This gives him a chance to get back and view his work with a new perspective. The change of pace refreshes him and helps him keep his perceptions sharp.

Harry also takes time off to be a parent and a grandparent. When Tim was just a boy, he and his neighborhood chums decided to put on a "circus act" and,

In a painting commissioned by the Church of Jesus Christ of Latter-day Saints, Anderson illustrates Isaiah prophesying the birth of the Messiah.

101

(Above) Following a design her husband made for her, Ruth Anderson did this magazine cover in needle point.

(Left) As He did on the hills of Galilee, Jesus draws simple but vital lessons from everyday life that give strength and guide the character of those who will listen to His voice.

(Overleaf) "May I Hold Him?" The appeal of the Christ-child to children is as strong today as ever.

103

further, to make a movie of it. Dad, ever patient, instead of discouraging such a grandiose scheme went right along with it and gave his aid. They dyed sheets and towels, and Father Anderson helped the boys cut out pennant-shaped flags to decorate their "ring." The circus never materialized but not for lack of parental support. Later, as a teen-ager, Tim bought an old model-T Ford that needed renovation. While he worked on the engine, his father worked on the body and the upholstering.

Nowadays it is Gabrielle, Kristin's daughter, who comes to "Bompa" for some sticks and boards "to make a music instrument." The resulting combination is her idea of a xylophone. Harry Anderson is as patient with her as with an art director who wants him to work in certain changes in a picture. His patience is not forced; it is his way of life.

A recent rendering of Christ in Gethsemane seeks to picture the trauma and pathos of that climactic hour.

SELFLESS
SERVICE

In 1962 Harry Anderson was awarded the Clara Obrig prize in the water-color division of the National Academy of Design in New York City, and was elected an associate of that body a few years later. He has consistently won awards from the American Watercolor Society (of which he is a member) and from the Art Directors Club. That he has not won more public honors is due to a consistently busy working schedule. Also, at the time of his conversion he made a deep commitment to serve his Lord and his church. Public recognition simply does not mean as much to him as it did earlier.

If he were willing to engage in artists' politics, wining and dining, and pulling strings, no doubt a wider path would have been beaten to his door. But then he probably would not be able to paint as he does, either, in a way that has such emotional impact upon men and women, boys and girls. For that matter, even those "important" guests who do come find Harry Anderson almost embarrassed if not unimpressed.

Even his own family has never heard him tell of winning a prize or of being elected to an honor society. His children would learn about it from their mother or perhaps read about it in the newspaper. Kristin grew up and was in college in another State before she realized the extent of her father's fame.

Nor has his family heard the artist say, "I did a good job," on any particular assignment. Harry gets his satisfaction simply from knowing within himself that he has done his best. He hasn't any "favorite" picture, and any painting that is more than five years old is not representa-

Love, virility, compassion, physical stamina, nobility, ultimate integrity—these are elements Anderson tries to portray in Jesus Christ.

tive of his work, he feels, for he is constantly seeking to improve on himself. "Almost every job I've sent out I've wished I had it back, for it was not as I wanted it—but I ran out of time in meeting a deadline."

One painting he did get back, but under unfortunate circumstances. The Review sent the famous "What Happened to Your Hand?" to an engraving company in Baltimore to have a new set of printing plates made. A fire broke out in the plant, and the painting became water-damaged. The Review sent the picture to Harry for re-working, but the models were no longer available and Harry's own style had changed.

Anderson believes he has yet to paint a "masterpiece" of the head and shoulders of Christ. Nor is he satisfied with any of his efforts to portray the Second Coming or the new earth. "I know so little about these subjects," he says. "Anything I do is only a subjective rendering; what they mean to me personally.

"I paint Christ the way I like Him, not to please other people. This is the way, if I met Him, I'd like to see Him. I've often wished I had lived in Jerusalem to see what He looked like. In the old days, painters used to portray Him as haggard, emaciated. The Bible says He would not stand out in a crowd, but it also suggests He was not ugly. I know He was a carpenter, that He did a lot of walking, so I see Him as strong, both physically and emotionally. I try to show that."

Anderson does not work on a picture with the express purpose of creating a certain feeling in the mind of the viewer. "There are so many different people, and each will view the picture from his or her own particular frame of reference. I have never known whether any of my pictures have done any good," he adds modestly, "and I may never know this side of heaven."

A devout student of the Word of God, Harry Anderson feels that no picture, alone, can effect a change in a person's religious life—that experience comes through Bible study and the ministry of the Holy Spirit. Pictures

© HARRY ANDERSON AND SAMUEL L. FELDMAN

Published here for the first time is Anderson's concept of the Last Supper—no ornateness, fine clothes, or composed countenances, but a humble room, foot-weary disciples in the grip of human emotions, and a Saviour on the brink of the world's destiny.

111

Ruth Anderson is an expert cook.

can internalize Bible truths, however, and impress them upon the memory. Moreover, Anderson's pictures have helped sell aids to Bible study, which in turn have led to spiritual commitments. Says Ruth, "We wouldn't think of a picture's going out without the prayer that it may be influential to some struggling soul."

The three hundred paintings Anderson has done for the Seventh-day Adventist Church, at prices well below market, constitute a major financial contribution in support of his faith. But he and his wife have not been content to let their commitment rest there. As Ruth puts it, "At our age, we are beginning to realize the scope of being Christian. All the warp and woof of life is involved in the cause of God."

The couple have always been strong supporters of

"God's Two Books." By the aid of the Holy Spirit, the Christ of the Bible can also be discerned in His handiwork. This painting called upon Anderson's skill at landscapes as well as his experience in depicting the face of Christ.

"Talking Wires." Telegraph lines spanning the continent spelled the end of the colorful saga of the Pony Express. This was a "Great Moment in American History," one of a series Anderson painted for Esso calendars.

Christian education. In Takoma Park the children attended a large and well-established elementary school operated by the church. The church school nearest to their New England home, however, was twenty-eight miles away. Ruth made this trip twice a day, five days a week, until Tim and then Kris had finished their elementary education. As they drove back and forth in their not-so-new Buick, they memorized Bible texts to help pass the miles. Later Kris attended and graduated from a

Anderson also painted the illustrations for several calendars featuring "Great Moments in American Motoring" for Esso, later Exxon. Shown is a 1930 Ruxton roadster.

denominationally operated liberal arts college in Massachusetts. She helped defray her tuition expense by working, first in the cafeteria and then by doing secretarial work.

Harry is first elder of the small church where he and Ruth are members. For many years he served as Sabbath school superintendent and often is called upon to teach a Bible class. Ruth plays the piano for the kindergarten division and sometimes teaches the adult Sabbath school

class. As first elder Harry is occasionally responsible for
the morning sermon. That he is willing to take the responsibility at all testifies to his dedication, for he does
not consider himself a teacher or public speaker; perspiration starts readily when he is "up front." But his
methodical, practical mind puts point to his message that
is not difficult for his New England audience to grasp.

Although the church is some fifteen miles from the
Anderson home—they chose it in part because they enjoy
the quiet ride on back-country roads—the couple are on
hand to help with any projects. The building itself is
quite old (it was rescued from demolishment by a society
interested in preserving old landmarks; the concert
soloist Marion Anderson was married in it), and the members gather for workbees to keep it in repair. Then there
is the annual Ingathering, or fund-raising campaign, and
board meetings in which Harry takes an active part.
Church officers and members often call on him for coun-
sel when the pastor, who lives in another town, is not
available.

The well-thumbed Bibles by Harry's bedside (he

commonly uses two—the Authorized Version and the Jerusalem Bible) testify to his own involvement in the Word of God. Yet he cherishes privacy in his personal relationship heavenward. Although he conducted family worship regularly when the children were home, those things he wanted most fervently he prayed for privately.

The family has had its share of problems. National recognition in his profession has paved no golden streets for them, nor spared them from human heartache. Harry, true to his profession, accepts shadow with sunshine and is happy with little as well as with much. But there have been times when Ruth was concerned about their daily bread. In the sixties came a period difficult for illustrators. Some of the national magazines that Anderson depended on to buy his work, such as *Saturday Evening Post* and *Woman's Home Companion,* were folding. Photography was being used more and more to illustrate both articles and advertisements. This not only meant less work for artists but increased the cost of models. As the artists had to raise their prices they found many of their buyers could no longer afford their work. Such was the case with the Review and Herald.

Harry gets to keep only about half the commission on any painting. The rest goes to model expense, photography and supplies, heat, and taxes, including Social Security. As a self-employed person Harry has to shoulder the full brunt of the latter. One expense he does not have is that of a public relations or sales agent, such as many artists utilize. "The Lord is our PR agent," Ruth explains. "He sends us business." That saves them 30 per cent on the price of each picture. However, the Andersons pay a tithe of their income to their church, in addition to regular freewill offerings. The total financial contribution, in one form or another, probably equals the expense that an agent would be to them.

In the mid-1960's Harry began receiving assignments from Esso and Humble Oil for calendar art and covers for road maps. The calendar assignments began as one or two pictures a year, in such series as "Great Moments in American History" (Anderson illustrated the opening of the Lancaster [Pennsylvania] Turnpike and the Discovery by Coronado of the Grand Canyon) and "Great Moments in Early American Motoring." Gradually these assignments increased until Harry was responsible for the entire calendar.

But there were pitfalls. At one point Harry, expecting another calendar assignment from Esso, set aside a block of time to accomplish it. Then the corporation changed its name to Exxon and canceled its calendars for that year. This left Anderson in the lurch. He filled in the time—and tried to aid his pocketbook—by painting various pictures and selling them at a showing at the local bank.

Medical problems and their attendant expenses have frequently been a drain on the Anderson resources—orthodontics, broken bones, bouts with pneumonia. When these coincided with periods of slack work, they were particularly onerous.

One summer Harry, Ruth, and Kristin drove to western Pennsylvania to visit Tim, then in college. Disliking turnpike food, Ruth had prepared a lunch, and they stopped in a parking lot at a turnpike restaurant to eat it. A man waiting nearby seemed to enjoy the sight of the family eating in their car, but Ruth, at the wheel, didn't appreciate his attention. Deciding suddenly to leave, she put the car in reverse gear and backed so quickly and unexpectedly that Harry lost hold of his potato salad and baked beans. But he didn't lose his temper. He only said quietly, "My food is in my lap." It is with that same equanimity that he accepts all the inconveniences and frustrations of life.

The Andersons rarely take a vacation. Ruth loves to travel, to get out and see new sights, meet new people, but Harry is content with the day-to-day work of his studio and garden. Besides, there's always a deadline to meet. Ruth may occasionally be tempted to take a little trip, arranging for a friend to accompany her, but always she gets to thinking of him, alone, shifting for himself, getting his own meals, and she hurries back home to be by his side. That is part of her contribution to the Harry Anderson success story.

118

NEW
DIMENSIONS

The New York World's Fair of 1964-1965 stirred the blood of many people, but for widely different reasons. While millions were making preparations to visit it and see the sights of the famous city as well, others were feverishly planning and building pavilions, booths, and displays to catch the attention of those millions of visitors.

Richard Marshall, of the Church of Jesus Christ of Latter-day Saints, made a call on Harry Anderson.

"The Mormon Church is planning a large display at the fair," he said. "We want to call attention, in the midst of all that commercialism, to the one answer of mankind's needs—Jesus Christ. We want to show by pictures the key points in His work for man, climaxing in His second coming. We have an artist here in the area working on it, and others elsewhere, but they will not be able to do all the pictures that we need in time for the fair. You have been recommended. Will you help us?"

Harry was happy to accept the assignment, if for no other reason than the challenges it presented. They wanted a picture five feet high and twelve feet long, done in oil. Harry had not used oils for more than thirty years, when he had discovered he was allergic to turpentine. But he had been wanting to get back into the medium if he could.

The painting was a picture of Jesus selecting His twelve disciples and ordaining them to preach the gospel of the kingdom. Anderson was happy to discover that by using varsol as a thinner, instead of turpentine, oil paints would not affect him as they used to do. He also learned

119

The first painting Harry Anderson did for the Mormon Church represented Christ ordaining His twelve disciples.

once again, however, that oils do not dry as quickly as casein paints. This made a difference in how much he could work in an area before he had to wait for the paint to dry. When the huge canvas was finished he hired a truck to haul it, on its stretcher, to New York where representatives of the Church of Jesus Christ of Latter-day Saints had a frame ready to display it at the main entrance of their pavilion.

The Mormons were happy with the job Harry did for them; they liked his style, the atmosphere about his paintings. They also liked the artist himself. They were ready to give him more picture assignments, all on Bible topics. And Harry returned the good will. The Mormons have a life-style that is similar in many respects to that of Seventh-day Adventists. Both bodies believe in a literal second coming of Jesus Christ, and this belief colors their philosophy, their approach to life. Mormons, like Adventists, endorse clean living; they do not indulge in

120

alcoholic beverages, tobacco, tea, or coffee. They are hard working, and they give high priority to happy homes and close family relationships.

Harry has painted a dozen or more large pictures for the Mormon Church, seven of them on the life of Christ. Others include Noah, Abraham, and the child Samuel hearing the voice of the Lord. Most of them hang in the Visitors' Center in Temple Square, Salt Lake City. Some, including a portrayal of the Second Coming, are in other centers. (There are twenty-five such centers around the world.) A picture of Jesus blessing the children hangs in the board room of the Board of Regents of Brigham Young University, which is, incidentally, the largest private university in the United States.

Several Harry Anderson paintings have been reproduced in selected publications of the Mormon Church. The *Family Home Evening* manual, of which 900,000 copies in seventeen languages are produced each year, features his pictures. When *Ensign,* general church paper for adults, used his unique portrayal of Jesus in Gethsemane on its cover and offered reprints to subscribers, forty thousand copies were sold. Church President Harold B. Lee used this picture one Christmas on his personal greeting cards.

The director for the church's public communications program, Wendell Ashton, enjoys his contacts and personal friendship with the Andersons. "I always feel a warmth in the Anderson home," Ashton says. "I find here the joy of simple and quiet living. I esteem not only Harry's paintings but also the love of Harry and Ruth.

"Harry has good priorities; he leads an undistracted life. I feel he keeps close to his Maker, and his own life comes through in his paintings. He puts a lot of spirituality into his pictures." Wendell also gives Harry the credit for the big tomatoes he grows—Harry taught him how to make and use compost.

For several years their Mormon friends pressed Harry and Ruth to visit Salt Lake City and see how his pictures were being displayed. Finally, in the summer of 1975, upon the invitation of President Spencer W. Kimball and his two counselors, the couple decided to go.

In the new thirty-story church office building in Salt Lake City is a mural that may become Harry Anderson's most well-known picture. Depicting Jesus commission-

ing His disciples just before His ascension, it measures sixteen feet high and sixty-six feet long. Grant Romney Clawson, an admirer of Harry Anderson and an artist in his own right, made the enlargement from a painting forty inches high and fourteen feet long. Every day thousands of people may be seen standing and admiring the mural. A reproduction of this picture also was used by the church for a brochure distributed to visitors.

The Visitors' Center nearby is the biggest tourist attraction in the entire Rocky Mountain area, outdrawing even Yellowstone National Park. Two and a half-million people pass through it each year. Here are featured most of Harry's paintings that he has done for the Mormons. When Ruth saw the picture of Isaiah prophesying the Messiah's birth, it took her breath away. She had seen it in her husband's studio, of course, but to see it in a proper

122

This painting of Christ giving His great commission to His disciples just before His ascension, has been reproduced in mural size, sixteen feet high and sixty-six feet long, in Salt Lake City.

setting and dramatically illuminated made her proud he'd done such a good work.

After spending several days in the Salt Lake City environs, the couple were driven by air-conditioned car on a tour of the State. The temperature reached as high as 104 degrees but because the humidity was low they didn't mind the heat. In fact, Ruth enjoyed the climate, and Harry, who normally does not like to travel, soon relaxed and enjoyed the trip.

They largely avoided the usual "tourist traps." Taking back roads, they visited mesas and canyons that, in their estimation, rival the Grand Canyon, not in size but in unexpected vistas. Harry reveled in the scenery; he took a large number of color pictures to use as background

123

Harry and Ruth.

material for paintings he hopes someday to do.

Only a few weeks after this the Andersons experienced another high light, of a slightly different nature. They were invited guests of a large convention of Seventh-day Adventist literature evangelists, meeting in Virginia. This group of men and women represented the thousands who, since the early 1940's, had been selling gospel literature made attractive in large measure by Harry's dedicated talent.

When introduced, the pair received a standing ovation that brought tears to their eyes. The warmth of their reception seemed to make up for the many days of labor and lonely nights spent in producing pictures.

After forty-five years of painting, Harry Anderson finds as much enjoyment in it as ever, and he has orders for at least a year's more work, with more orders coming in. But he is looking forward to the time when he can paint what *he* wants to, rather than what an art director wants. And what would that be? He has always had a preference for landscapes—he likes to paint nature. Now that he has had a taste of the West he wants to paint Western scenes. Ruth likes the climate there; perhaps they could move.

Would there be no people in his Western pictures? Yes, there would be people—common people. Andrew Loomis, in his book *Figure Drawing for All It's Worth,* encourages art students to develop any natural interest along specific lines; it will help them to focus their abilities toward success. He uses Harry Anderson to illustrate his point: "Harry Anderson loves plain American people —the old family doctor, the little white cottage."

Harry Anderson would include himself among "plain American people." But on the other hand he has helped a lot of other people rise above their level, to lift their sights above their problems. Through his brush he has introduced them to the Saviour he knows, the compassionate yet capable Jesus.

A PERSONAL
MESSAGE

Harry's paintings may be found all over the world. Prints of "What Happened to Your Hand?" or of "May I Hold Him?" may be found on the bedroom walls of teen-agers in Europe or South America. New Christians in an African or Asian village right now may be studying a "picture roll," consisting largely of Harry's religious pictures.

After studying and loving these pictures, many of these people want to know more about the artist, whose signature they find, usually in the lower right hand corner. So I would like to share with the reader some of the qualities I find in him. While numerous magazine articles have been written about him, relating to his career and his hobbies, not much has been said about his relationship with his family. But this latter aspect is important; it reveals much about a person's character as well as his personality. Almost forty years of marriage is some indication that we love each other. Let me tell you what I like about him.

Harry is a low-keyed, quiet, unassuming man, with an innate sense of politeness and consideration for his family, as well as for friends and guests. That is not to say that he always remembers to open a door for me, or to help me out of a car—those attentions are somewhat superficial, anyway. What is more important to me is that he does not force his ideas or wishes upon me. I thrive in what I call an atmosphere of benign domination. Although I ask his advice in a matter, I like to be free to make my own decisions. But by experience, including some unusual ones, I have found that when I abide by his

126

practical advice I benefit immensely.

Harry is a compassionate man, fair in his judgments, tender and gentle. When I call him to lunch he will often come bringing a handful of wildflowers he has picked for me. Any woman who is fond of flowers will cherish such attention. He is a supportive husband and father, enthusiastic about the individual projects of family members, ready to help us when we encounter hard spots.

That one should be talented in so many ways might be depressing to others of lesser talents. But because he is not burdened by self-importance or excessive egotism, he does not make us of smaller gifts feel inferior or frustrated.

Harry's positive outlook, his love for challenges, his ability to come up with alternatives as necessary, contributes to his youthful spirit. To share life with such a person has been a great blessing. That gentle man has made life more meaningful and creative for me.

—Ruth Anderson